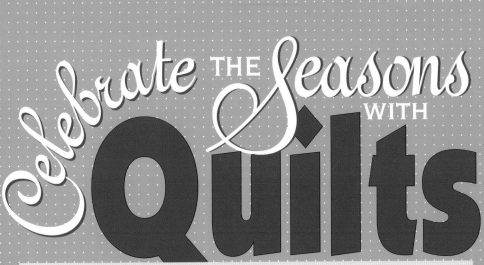

Celebrate THE Seasons WITH Quilts

from the editors of Traditional Quiltworks *and* Quilting Today *magazines*

CHITRA PUBLICATIONS

Your Best Value in Quilting

www.QuiltTownUSA.com

D1119457

First Printing: 2001
Library of Congress Cataloging-in-Publication Data

Celebrate the seasons with quilts / from the editors of Traditional quiltworks
and Quilting today magazines.
        p. cm.
    ISBN 1-885588-37-2
    1. Patchwork—Patterns. 2. Patchwork quilts. 3. Seasons in
art. I. Traditional quiltworks. II. Quilting today.
    TT835 .C413 2001
    746.46'041—dc21   00-065902

Edited by: Elsie Campbell
Design and Illustrations: Brenda Pytlik
Photography: Van Zandbergen Photography, Brackney, Pennsylvania and
Stephen J. Appel Photography, Vestal, New York
Cover Design by Diane Albeck-Grick

Our Mission Statement:

*We publish quality quilting magazines and books that recognize,
promote, and inspire self-expression. We are dedicated to serving
our customers with respect, kindness, and efficiency.*

Introduction

When you view a quilt, can you easily pick a season that the colors and design represent? Most people find something in each quilt they view that triggers a memory. The earthy colors of red, orange, yellow, brown, and green are reminiscent of fall and may evoke memories of warm autumn afternoons spent raking piles of leaves in the yard and the smell of smoke in the air. Pastel colors, like those found in feedsacks which were used to make quilts during the 1930's, may remind you of spring flowers—the wild yellow of daffodils or deep lavenders of crocus, for example. How about the many bright colors of tulips in full bloom as a reminder of spring? And then there are quilts in the lively red and green colors that we associate with the Christmas season.

Do you have a favorite time of year? Even when that season passes, you can keep the atmosphere alive year-round with a quilt to hang on a wall or display on a bed. If you love them all, make several quilts, each in the colors and patterns of a single season, and rotate them to dress your bed to reflect the weather outside.

The twelve quilts in this book were carefully selected from among our favorites. Each colorful design is a treat to look at and fun to make. So, take a little time between your seasonal chores to enjoy stitching one of these delightful, yet simple-to-make, quilts.

The Editors of
Traditional Quiltworks and
Quilting Today magazines

The editorial team, clockwise from the top, Jack Braunstein, Debra Feece, Deborah Hearn, Elsie Campbell, and Joyce Libal

Contents

*The patterns are rated for difficulty.
Look for these symbols with every pattern.*
🪣 Beginner   🪣🪣 Intermediate

Child's Play

It's just a hop, skip, and a jump to make this delightful spring-time quilt.

QUILT SIZE: 39" x 52"
BLOCK SIZE: 3" square

MATERIALS
- Assorted light to medium prints totaling one yard
- Assorted dark prints totaling one yard
- 3/8 yard white polka dot
- 3/8 yard light pink print
- 3/8 yard medium pink print
- 3/4 yard dark pink print
- 1 5/8 yards backing fabric
- 43" x 56" piece of batting

CUTTING
For each of 72 Block A's:
- Cut 5: 1 1/2" squares, light to medium print
- Cut 4: 1 1/2" squares, dark print
For each of 36 Block B's:
- Cut 5: 1 1/2" squares, dark print
- Cut 4: 1 1/2" squares, light to medium print
Also:
- Cut 28: 3 1/2" squares, white polka dot
- Cut 26: 3 1/2" squares, light pink print
- Cut 34: 3 1/2" squares, medium pink print
- Cut 10: 5 1/2" squares, dark pink print, then cut them in quarters diagonally to yield 40 setting triangles. You will use 38.
- Cut 2: 3" squares, dark pink print, then cut them in half diagonally to yield 4 corner triangles
- Cut 5: 2 1/2" x 44" strips, dark pink print, for the binding

DIRECTIONS
For each Block A:
- Lay out five 1 1/2" light to medium print squares and four 1 1/2" dark print squares. Sew them into rows, as shown, and join the rows to make a Nine Patch block. Make 72.

For each Block B:
- Lay out five 1 1/2" dark print squares and four 1 1/2" light to medium print squares. Sew them into rows, as shown, and join the rows to make a Nine Patch block. Make 36.

ASSEMBLY
- Referring to the quilt photo and the Assembly Diagram, lay out the A and B blocks, 3 1/2" white polka dot squares, 3 1/2" light pink print squares, 3 1/2" medium pink print squares, and the dark pink print setting and corner triangles.

Assembly Diagram

- Sew them into diagonal rows and join the rows.
- Finish the quilt as described in the *General Directions*, using the 2 1/2" x 44" dark pink print strips for the binding.

Lisa Mansfield of Tulsa, Okalahoma, used a variety of scrappy Nine Patch blocks obtained from members of her guild to make this springtime quilt. Lisa used reproduction fabrics in shades of pink for the alternate squares in **"Child's Play"** *(39" x 52"), an appropriate name because this quilt is so quick and easy to construct.*

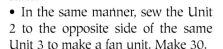

Spring

Friendship Fan

Soft pastel print fans whisper gentle spring breezes.

QUILT SIZE: 69" x 81"
BLOCK SIZE: 12" square

MATERIALS
- 3 1/2 yards muslin
- Assorted scraps of light and medium pastel prints each at least 4 1/2" x 10" and totaling 3 1/2 yards
- 2 1/2 yards pink
- 1/3 yard yellow
- 4 yards backing fabric
- 73" x 85" piece of thin batting

CUTTING
Cut the lengthwise strips before cutting other pieces from the same yardage.
- Cut 30: A, assorted prints
- Cut 30: AR, assorted prints
- Cut 60: B, assorted prints
- Cut 60: BR, assorted prints
- Cut 2: 4 1/2" x 86" lengthwise strips, pink, for the border
- Cut 2: 4 1/2" x 74" lengthwise strips, pink, for the border
- Cut 5: 2 1/2" x 65" lengthwise strips, pink, for the binding
- Cut 15: C, pink
- Cut 15: C, yellow
- Cut 30: D, muslin

DIRECTIONS
- Sew a print A to a print B to make Unit 1. Make 30.
- Sew a print AR to a print BR to make Unit 2. Make 30.

- Sew a print B to a print BR to make Unit 3. Make 30.

- Lay a Unit 3 on a Unit 1, right sides together. Start stitching at the narrow end, stop 1/4" from the wide end and backstitch.
- In the same manner, sew the Unit 2 to the opposite side of the same Unit 3 to make a fan unit. Make 30.

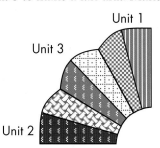

- Place a fan unit on a pink C, right sides together, aligning the small curve of the fan unit with the curved edge of the pink C. Place a pin in the center and at each edge, as shown.

- Sew the fan unit to the pink C, manipulating the curves to align the edges as you sew. Make 15.

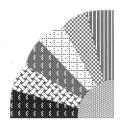

- Sew a fan unit to a yellow C in the same manner. Make 15.

- Place a muslin D on the opposite edge of a fan unit, right sides together, aligning the inner points and curves, and placing pins at each edge, at both inner points, and in the center of each curve, as shown.

- Sew the muslin D to the fan unit, manipulating the curves to align the edges and pivoting at the inner points to complete a Fan block. Make 30.

- Referring to the quilt photo, lay out the Fan blocks in 6 rows of 5. Sew the blocks into rows and join the rows.
- Center and sew a 4 1/2" x 86" pink strip to each long side of the quilt. Start, stop, and backstitch 1/4" from each edge.
- In the same manner, center and sew a 4 1/2" x 74" pink strip to each short side of the quilt.
- Miter the corners as described in the *General Directions*.
- Finish the quilt as described in the *General Directions*, using the 2 1/2" x 65" pink strips for the binding.

(Full-size pattern pieces for "Friendship Fan" are on page 29.)

Spring is in the air! **"Friendship Fan"** *(69" x 81"), is Patricia Reid's charming quilt made of fabrics she bought from, and swapped with, fellow members of the Feedsack Club. After the Florida quiltmaker machine pieced her blocks, she wrote the names of the friends who provided the fabric on the fan handles. New muslin provides a light background, and pink borders complete the springtime atmosphere created by this quilt.*

Spring

Yard Sale Tulips

Spring means tulips, especially with this simple-to-appliqué quilt!

QUILT SIZE: 53" x 66"
BLOCK SIZE: 13" square

MATERIALS
- 4 yards white
- 1 1/3 yards yellow
- 5/8 yard green
- 4 yards backing fabric
- 57" x 70" piece of batting

CUTTING
Appliqué pattern pieces are full size and do not include a seam allowance. Make templates for each of the pattern pieces. Trace around the templates on the right side of the fabrics and add a 1/8" to 3/16" turn-under allowance when cutting the pieces out. All other dimensions include a 1/4" seam allowance. Cut the lengthwise strips before cutting other pieces from the same yardage.
- Cut 3: 2 1/2" x 90" lengthwise strips, white, for the binding
- Cut 20: 14" squares, white
- Cut 20: 1 3/8" x 5 3/8" strips, green
- Cut 40: C, green
- Cut 20: A, yellow
- Cut 20: B, yellow
- Cut 20: BR, yellow

DIRECTIONS
For each of 20 blocks:
- Press both long edges of a 1 3/8" x 5 3/8" green strip 1/4" to the wrong side to prepare a stem.

- Center the stem on a 14" white square, placing one end of the stem 1/4" from the bottom edge, as shown.

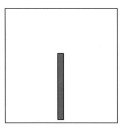

- Appliqué the pressed edges of the stem to the square.
- Place a yellow A on the square with the bottom edge meeting the stem. Pin it in place and appliqué the upper edges to the square.

- Pin a yellow B to the square, overlapping the left side of the A and the upper edge of the green stem. Appliqué it in place.

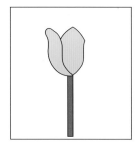

- In the same manner, appliqué a yellow BR to the square, overlapping the right side of the A. NOTE: *You may want to trim the turn-under allowances slightly at the lower edges of the appliqué pieces to reduce bulk.*
- Referring to the quilt photo, appliqué a green leaf (C) to the square on one side of the stem. Repeat for the remaining leaf on the opposite side of the stem.

- Trim the block to 13 1/2" square, keeping the tulip centered.

ASSEMBLY
- Lay out the blocks in 5 rows of 4. Sew the blocks into rows and join the rows.
- Finish the quilt as described in the *General Directions*, using the 2 1/2" x 90" white strips for the binding.

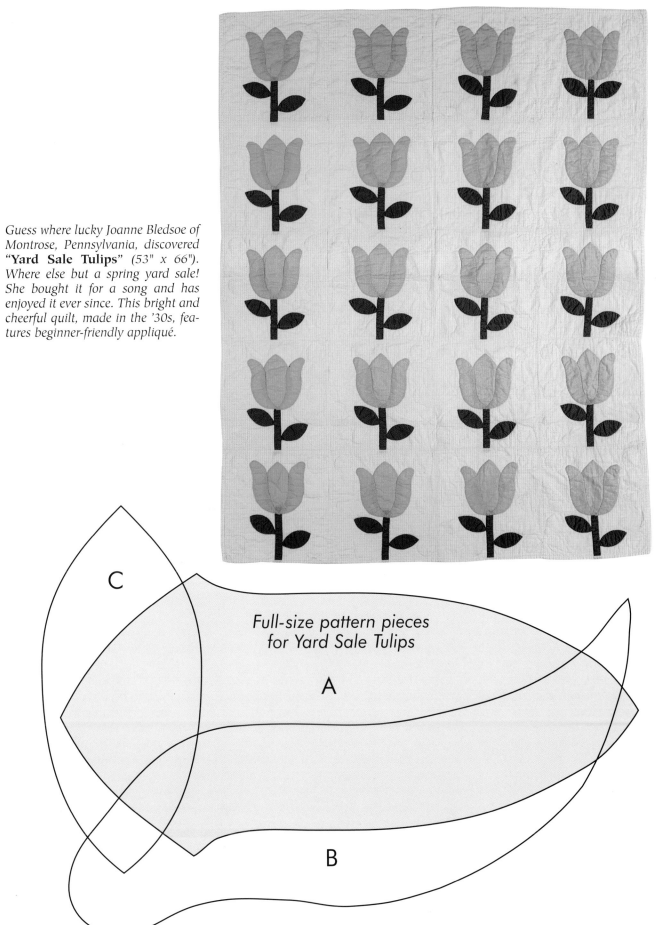

Guess where lucky Joanne Bledsoe of Montrose, Pennsylvania, discovered **"Yard Sale Tulips"** (53" x 66"). Where else but a spring yard sale! She bought it for a song and has enjoyed it ever since. This bright and cheerful quilt, made in the '30s, features beginner-friendly appliqué.

C

Full-size pattern pieces for Yard Sale Tulips

A

B

9

Summer

Butterfly Ballet

Appliqué a recital of graceful butterflies.

QUILT SIZE: 76 1/2" x 96"
BLOCK SIZE: 18" square

MATERIALS
- Assorted scraps of light, medium, and dark prints each at least 8" square for the wings
- Assorted scraps of light, medium, and dark prints each at least 4" x 6" for the spots
- 3/8 yard black print for the butterfly bodies
- 3 1/4 yards muslin
- 3 5/8 yards yellow print
- 1/2 yard green print
- 5/8 yard pink print
- 5 1/2 yards backing fabric
- 81" x 100" piece of batting
- Black embroidery floss

CUTTING
Appliqué pattern pieces are full size and do not include a seam allowance. Make templates for each of the pattern pieces. Trace around the templates on the right side of the fabrics and add a 1/8" to 3/16" turn-under allowance when cutting the pieces out. Cut the lengthwise strips before cutting other pieces from the same yardage. All other dimensions include a 1/4" seam allowance.

For each of 48 butterflies:
- Cut 1: A, light, medium, or dark print
- Cut 1: AR, same print
- Cut 1: B, same print
- Cut 1: BR, same print
- Cut 2: C, contrasting print
- Cut 2: D, same contrasting print
- Cut 1: E, black print

Also:
- Cut 12: 18 1/2" squares, muslin
- Cut 2: 3" x 98" lengthwise strips,

yellow print, for the outer border
- Cut 2: 3" x 72" lengthwise strips, yellow print, for the outer border
- Cut 2: 3 1/4" x 88" lengthwise strips, yellow print
- Cut 8: 3 1/4" x 18 1/2" lengthwise strips, yellow print, for the vertical sashing
- Cut 5: 3 1/4" x 60" lengthwise strips, yellow print, for the horizontal sashing
- Cut 9: 2 1/2" x 44" crosswise strips, yellow print, for the binding
- Cut 8: 1 3/4" x 44" strips, green print, for the inner border
- Cut 8: 2" x 44" strips, pink print, for the middle border

DIRECTIONS
For each of 12 blocks:
- Fold an 18 1/2" muslin square in quarters diagonally. Lightly press the folds.
- Using a pencil and a light box or brightly lit window, trace the butterfly design on each corner of the 18 1/2" muslin square, aligning the center of the butterfly body with the fold lines. Keep the design 2" from the edges of the square.
- Use the tip of your needle to turn under the allowance as you appliqué a print A and a matching print AR in place. There is no need to turn under the allowance where pieces will be overlapped. Appliqué a print B and BR in place, overlapping the A and AR, as shown.

- Appliqué the contrasting print C's and D's on the butterfly wings.
- Appliqué a black print E, overlapping the inner edges of the wings.
- Appliqué a butterfly to each remaining corner of the muslin square in the same manner.
- Using 3 strands of black embroidery floss, stitch antenna on each butterfly with an outline stitch.

ASSEMBLY
- Referring to the quilt photo, lay out 3 blocks alternately with two 3 1/4" x 18 1/2" yellow print strips and stitch them into a row. Make 4.
- Sew 3 1/4" x 60" yellow print strips between the rows and at the top and bottom.
- Measure the length of the quilt. Trim the 3 1/4" x 88" yellow print strips to that measurement. Sew them to the long sides of the quilt.
- Sew the 1 3/4" x 44" green print strips together, end to end, to make a long pieced strip.
- Measure the width of the quilt. Cut 2 lengths from the long pieced strip each equal to that measurement, and stitch them to the short sides of the quilt.
- Measure the length of the quilt, including the borders. Cut 2 lengths from the long pieced strip each equal to that measurement, and stitch them to the long sides of the quilt.
- Sew the 2" x 44" pink print strips together, end to end, to make a long pieced strip.
- In the same manner as for the green print strips, cut 2 lengths from the pieced strip to fit the quilt's width, and stitch them to the short sides of the quilt.

Peggy Kraum-Brown of Bonner Springs, Kansas, remembers ballet lessons when she was a child. Her mother once sewed beautiful butterfly costumes of satins, sequins, and lace for her recital. Peggy and her class-mates danced as if in flight to the music. **"Butterfly Ballet"** (76 1/2" x 96") reminds her of that happy time. Make your version to remind you of summertime delights.

- Cut 2 lengths from the pieced strip to fit the quilt's length, and stitch them to the long sides of the quilt.
- Trim the 3" x 72" yellow print strips to fit the quilt's width, and stitch them to the short sides of the quilt.
- Trim the 3" x 98" yellow print strips to fit the quilt's length, and stitch them to the long sides of the quilt.
- Finish the quilt as described in the *General Directions*, using the 2 1/2" x 44" yellow print strips for the binding.

Full-size pattern pieces for Butterfly Ballet (Flip the wings and add them to the other side of the butterfly body to complete the design.)

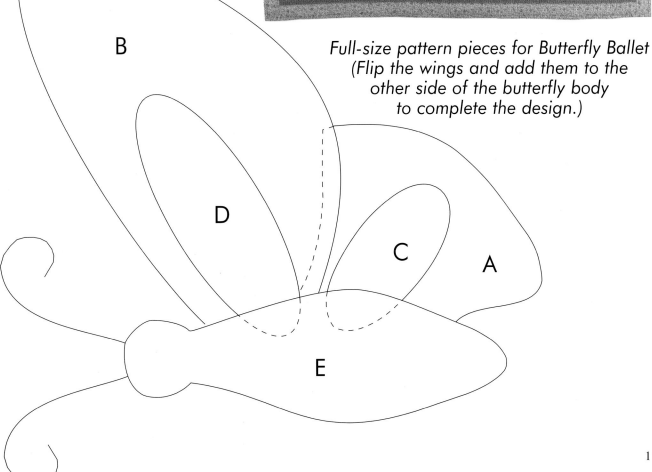

B

D

C

A

E

Summer

Houses

 *Use patriotic colors to piece a neighborhood of summer fun!*

QUILT SIZE: 78" x 101"
BLOCK SIZE: 12" square

MATERIALS
- Fat eighth (11" x 18") each of 24 assorted prints for the houses
- 2 yards muslin
- 3 yards navy ticking stripe
- 3/4 yard navy print
- 1 yard red check for the side borders NOTE: *The yardage given is for pieced borders. If you prefer to cut them from one length of fabric, you will need 3 yards*
- 1 yard red plaid for the binding
- 6 yards backing fabric
- 82" x 105" piece of batting

CUTTING
Cut pieces A, B, C, H, I, J, K, L and M using your rotary cutter and ruler. Pattern pieces D, E, F and G (on page 30) are full size and include a 1/4" seam allowance, as do all dimensions given. Label all pieces as indicated.

From each house print:
- Cut 2: 1 1/2" x 2 1/2" rectangles (B)
- Cut 1: 2 1/2" x 5 1/2" strip (C)
- Cut 1: E
- Cut 1: G
- Cut 2: 1 1/2" x 6 1/2" strips (I)
- Cut 2: 2" x 5" strips (J)
- Cut 2: 1 3/4" x 4" strips (L)
- Cut 1: 1 1/2" x 4" strip (M)

From the muslin:
- Cut 48: 2 1/2" x 3" rectangles (A)
- Cut 24: 2 1/2" x 5 1/2" strips (C)
- Cut 24: D
- Cut 24: DR
- Cut 24: F
- Cut 24: 1 1/2" x 7" strips (H)
- Cut 24: 1 1/2" x 6 1/2" strips (I)
- Cut 24: 2 1/2" x 5" strips (K)
- Cut 48: 1 3/4" x 4" strips (L)

Also:
- Cut 58: 4 1/2" x 12 1/2" strips, navy ticking stripe with the stripes running lengthwise in the strips
- Cut 35: 4 1/2" squares, navy print, for the cornerstones
- Cut 5: 6" x 44" strips, red check, for the side borders
- Cut 10: 2 1/2" x 44" strips, red plaid, for the binding

DIRECTIONS
For each of 24 House blocks:
- Lay out 2 muslin A's, 2 print B's, and a muslin C. NOTE: *Use one print for each House block.* Sew them together to make a chimney section, as shown. Set it aside.

- Sew a muslin F between a print E and a print G. NOTE: *Match the dots on the pattern pieces for proper alignment.*

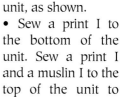

- Sew a muslin D and a muslin DR to the unit to make a roof section. Set it aside.

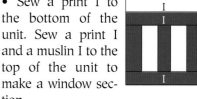

- Sew a muslin K between 2 print J's. Sew a print C to the top of the unit. Sew a muslin H to the right side to make a door section. Set it aside.

- Lay out 2 muslin L's, 2 print L's, and a print M. Sew them together to make a unit, as shown.
- Sew a print I to the bottom of the unit. Sew a print I and a muslin I to the top of the unit to make a window section.
- Lay out the 4 sections. Join the door and window sections. Join the chimney and roof sections.
- Sew the 2 pieced units together to complete a House block.

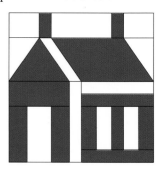

ASSEMBLY
- Referring to the quilt photo, lay out 4 House blocks and five 4 1/2" x 12 1/2" navy ticking strips. Sew them together to make a House row. Make 6.
- Lay out four 4 1/2" x 12 1/2" navy ticking strips and five 4 1/2" navy print squares. Join them to make a pieced sashing strip. Make 7.
- Lay out the pieced sashing strips and House rows, beginning and ending with a pieced sashing strip. Sew them together.
- Sew the 6" x 44" red check strips together, end to end, to make a long pieced strip.

Bette Nasser Clark of Montrose, Pennsylvania, was the lucky winner of a set of House blocks made by her fellow Stitch 'n Time guild members. Bette pieced some additional blocks and assembled "Houses" (78" x 101"), her first full-size quilt. Cool and crisp, the ticking stripe sashings and checked borders lend an old-fashioned country summer look to this quilt.

- Measure the length of the quilt. Trim 2 lengths from the long pieced strip each equal to that measurement.
- Sew them to the sides of the quilt.

- Finish the quilt as described in the *General Directions*, using the 2 1/2" x 44" red plaid strips for the binding.

(Full-size pattern pieces for "Houses" are on page 30.)

Sailboats

Bright, colorful boats sail across this charming summertime quilt.

QUILT SIZE: 65" x 93"
BLOCK SIZE: 12" square

MATERIALS
- 1/8 yard each of 24 assorted prints
- 2 1/2 yards white
- 1/2 yard blue print
- 1 1/2 yards purple plaid
- 1/4 yard red plaid
- 2 1/2 yards turquoise print
- 6 yards backing fabric
- 69" x 97" piece of batting

CUTTING
For each of 24 Sailboat blocks:
- Cut 2: 3 1/2" squares, print
- Cut 3: 3 7/8" squares, same print

Also:
- Cut 72: 3 7/8" squares, white
- Cut 96: 3 1/2" squares, white
- Cut 8: 2 1/2" x 44" strips, white, for the binding
- Cut 24: 3 1/2" x 12 1/2" strips, blue print, for the water
- Cut 58: 2 1/2" x 12 1/2" strips, purple plaid, for the sashing
- Cut 35: 2 1/2" squares, red plaid, for the cornerstones
- Cut 2: 3 1/2" x 88" lengthwise strips, turquoise print, for the border
- Cut 2: 3 1/2" x 66" lengthwise strips, turquoise print, for the border

PREPARATION
- Draw a diagonal line from corner to corner on the wrong side of each 3 7/8" white square, as shown.

DIRECTIONS
For each of 24 Sailboat blocks:
- Place a marked 3 7/8" white square on a 3 7/8" print square, right sides together. Stitch 1/4" away from the diagonal line

on both sides, as shown. Make 3.
- Cut the squares on the drawn lines to yield 6 pieced squares.
- Lay out the pieced squares, the 3 1/2" matching print squares and four 3 1/2" white squares in 3 rows of 4. Stitch them into rows and join the rows to make a pieced unit, as shown.
- Stitch a 3 1/2" x 12 1/2" blue print strip to the bottom of the pieced unit, as shown, to complete a Sailboat block.

ASSEMBLY
- Lay out the 24 Sailboat blocks, the 2 1/2" x 12 1/2" purple plaid sashing strips, and the 2 1/2" red plaid squares, as shown in the Assembly Diagram.
- Stitch the Sailboat blocks and the vertical sashing strips into horizontal rows.
- Stitch the horizontal sashing strips and cornerstones into rows.
- Join the rows.
- Measure the length of the quilt. Trim the 3 1/2" x 88" turquoise print strips to that measurement. Stitch them to the sides of the quilt.
- Measure the width of the quilt, including the borders. Trim the 3 1/2" x 66" turquoise print strips to that measurement. Stitch them to the top and bottom of the quilt.
- Finish the quilt as described in the *General Directions*, using the 2 1/2" x 44" white strips for the binding.

Assembly Diagram

14

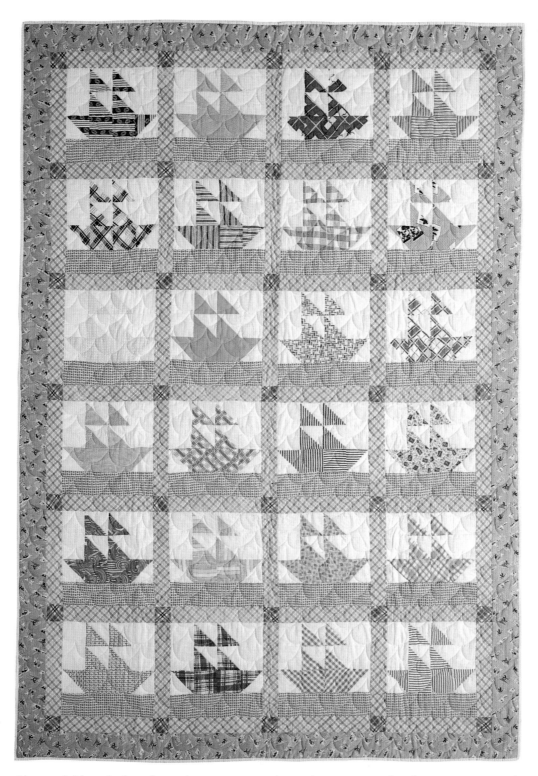

Just as children flock to the park in summer, quilters turn to sunny colors for summertime quilts. Connie Tilman of Powhatan, Virginia, stitched bright, colorful sailboats afloat on rivers of blue in **"Sailboats"** *(65" x 93"). Connie is a member of the Feedsack Club and enjoys using cheerful feedsack fabrics in her quilts. Make your version using your favorite fabrics.*

Autumn

Geese in the Barn

Flying Geese and Log Cabins combine beautifully in this autumn-inspired quilt.

QUILT SIZE: 86 1/2" square
BLOCK SIZE: 9" square

MATERIALS

- 1/8 yard red print
- Assorted light prints totaling at least 1 5/8 yards
- Assorted brown prints totaling at least 1 3/4 yards
- Assorted blue prints ranging from teal through purple totaling at least 4 1/2 yards
- 4 3/4 yards beige
- 3/4 yard navy print for the binding
- 7 3/4 yards backing fabric
- 91" square of batting

CUTTING

From the assorted light prints:

- Cut 36: 1 1/2" squares
- Cut 36: 1 1/2" x 2 1/2" strips
- Cut 36: 1 1/2" x 3 1/2" strips
- Cut 36: 1 1/2" x 4 1/2" strips
- Cut 36: 1 1/2" x 5 1/2" strips
- Cut 36: 1 1/2" x 6 1/2" strips
- Cut 36: 1 1/2" x 7 1/2" strips
- Cut 36: 1 1/2" x 8 1/2" strips

From the assorted brown prints:

- Cut 36: 1 1/2" x 2 1/2" strips
- Cut 36: 1 1/2" x 3 1/2" strips
- Cut 36: 1 1/2" x 4 1/2" strips
- Cut 36: 1 1/2" x 5 1/2" strips
- Cut 36: 1 1/2" x 6 1/2" strips
- Cut 36: 1 1/2" x 7 1/2" strips
- Cut 36: 1 1/2" x 8 1/2" strips
- Cut 36: 1 1/2" x 9 1/2" strips

From the assorted blue prints:

- Cut 336: 2 3/4" x 5" rectangles
- Cut 49: 5" squares

Also:

- Cut 868: 2 3/4" squares, beige
- Cut 36: 1 1/2" squares, red print
- Cut 9: 2 1/2" x 44" strips, navy, for the binding

DIRECTIONS

- Sew a 1 1/2" red print square to a 1 1/2" light print square, right sides together. Continue chain sewing the remaining 1 1/2" red print squares to the 1 1/2" light print squares, as shown. Cut the units apart and press the seam allowances toward the light print.
- Lay a unit right side up with the light print square toward the bottom. Place a 1 1/2" x 2 1/2" light print strip on the unit, right side down. Sew them together. Chain sew 1 1/2" x 2 1/2" light print strips to the remaining units in the same manner. Cut the units apart and press the seam allowances toward the last strip added.
- Lay a unit right side up with the last strip added toward the bottom. Place a 1 1/2" x 2 1/2" brown print strip on the unit, right side down. Sew them together. Chain sew 1 1/2" x 2 1/2" brown print strips to the remaining units. Cut the units apart and press the seam allowances toward the last strip added.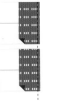
- Lay a unit right side up with the last strip added toward the bottom. Place a 1 1/2" x 3 1/2" brown print strip on the unit, right side down. Sew them together. Chain piece the remaining units. Clip them apart and press the seam allowances toward the last strip added, as before.

- Continue adding strips to the units in the same manner to complete 36 Log Cabin blocks, as shown. Set them aside.

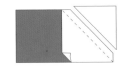

- Draw a diagonal line from corner to corner on the wrong side of each 2 3/4" beige square. NOTE: *If you prefer, press the 2 3/4" beige squares in half diagonally, wrong side in, instead of marking them.*
- Place a marked square on one end of a 2 3/4" x 5" blue print rectangle, right sides together. Sew on the drawn or pressed line, as shown. Press the beige square toward the corner, aligning the edges. Trim the seam allowance to 1/4".

- Place a marked beige square on the opposite end of the rectangle. Sew on the drawn or pressed line, as shown. Press and trim, as before, to complete a Flying Geese unit. Make 336.

*Charlotte Roach of Stratford, Connecticut, made "**Geese in the Barn**" (86 1/2" square) after taking a tour through an old barn. Birds flying in and out of the barn inspired her to combine two traditional blocks. The Flying Geese in the sashing appear to float over a background of Log Cabin blocks, giving a three dimensional feel to this fall quilt.*

• Sew 4 Flying Geese units into a row, as shown. Make 84. Set them aside.
• Place a marked beige print square on one corner of a 5" blue print square. Sew on the drawn line. Press toward the corner and trim, as before. Repeat for the remaining corners to make a Square-in-a-Square unit. Make 49.

ASSEMBLY
• Lay out 6 Log Cabin blocks and 7 Flying Geese rows, as shown. Join them to make a row. Make 4.

• Lay out 6 Log Cabin blocks and 7 Flying Geese rows, as shown. Join them to make a row. Make 2.

• Lay out 6 Flying Geese rows and 7 Square-in-a-Square units, as shown. Sew them together to make a sashing row. Make 4.

• Lay out 6 Flying Geese rows and 7 Square-in-a-Square units, as shown. Sew them together to make an alternate sashing row. Make 3.

• Referring to the quilt photo, lay out the block rows and sashing rows. Sew them together.
• Finish the quilt as described in the *General Directions*, using the 2 1/2" x 44" navy strips for the binding.

Autumn

Maple Leaf

The seasonal colors of falling leaves are reflected in this scrappy patchwork quilt.

QUILT SIZE: 83" x 102 1/2"
BLOCK SIZE: 12" square

MATERIALS

• Assorted prints and solids in fall leaf colors totaling 2 3/4 yards
• 4 yards off-white for the blocks, setting and corner triangles, and the binding
• 3 1/2 yards brown for the stems and sashing strips
• 6 yards backing fabric
• 87" x 107" piece of batting

CUTTING

The appliqué piece (A) on page 30 is full size and does not include a seam allowance. Make a template for the pattern piece. Trace around the template on the right side of the fabric and add a 1/8" to 3/16" turn-under allowance when cutting the pieces out. Cut the lengthwise strips before cutting other pieces from the same yardage.

• Cut 736: 2 1/2" squares, assorted prints and solids
• Cut 224: 2 1/2" x 4 1/2" rectangles, off-white
• Cut 96: 2 1/2" squares, off-white
• Cut 32: 4 1/2" squares, off-white
• Cut 4: 21" squares, off-white, then cut them in quarters diagonally to yield 16 setting triangles. You will use 14.
• Cut 2: 12 1/4" squares, off-white, then cut them in half diagonally to yield 4 corner triangles
• Cut 10: 2 1/2" x 44" strips, off-white, for the binding
• Cut 1: 2 1/2" x 116" lengthwise strip, brown, for the sashing
• Cut 2: 2 1/2" x 104" lengthwise strips, brown for the sashing
• Cut 2: 2 1/2" x 76" lengthwise

strips, brown, for the sashing
• Cut 2: 2 1/2" x 48" lengthwise strips, brown, for the sashing
• Cut 2: 2 1/2" x 20" lengthwise strips, brown, for the sashing
• Cut 40: 2 1/2" x 12 1/2" strips, brown, for the sashing
• Cut 32: A, brown, for the stems

DIRECTIONS

For each of 32 Maple Leaf blocks:

• Draw a diagonal line from corner to corner on the wrong side of each of 8 assorted print or solid 2 1/2" squares. NOTE: *If you prefer, press the 2 1/2" squares in half diagonally, wrong side in, instead of marking them.*
• Place a marked square on one end of a 2 1/2" x 4 1/2" off-white rectangle, right sides together. Sew on the drawn or pressed line, as shown. Press the square toward the corner, aligning the edges. Trim the seam allowance to 1/4".
• Place a marked square on the opposite end of the rectangle. Sew on the drawn or pressed line. Press and trim as before, to complete a Flying Geese unit. Make 4.
• Stitch two 2 1/2" assorted print or solid squares together to make a pieced rectangle, as shown. Make 6.
• Stitch a pieced rectangle to a Flying Geese unit to make a pieced side square, as shown. Make 4.

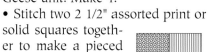

• Stitch 2 pieced rectangles together to make a Four Patch unit.

• Stitch a 2 1/2" assorted print or solid square to a 2 1/2" off-white square. Sew this pieced unit to a 2 1/2" x 4 1/2" off-white rectangle to make a corner square. Make 3.

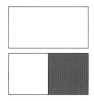

• Appliqué a brown A (stem) to a 4 1/2" off-white square, as shown.

• Lay out 4 pieced side squares, the Four-patch unit, 3 corner squares and the stem square in 3 rows of 3, as shown. Stitch the squares into rows and join the rows to complete a Maple Leaf block.

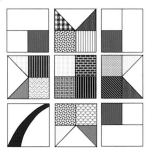

(Continued on page 28)

Margot Cohen of Cedarhurst, New York, used a full spectrum of autumn-colored fabrics for her **"Maple Leaf Quilt"** *(83" x 102 1/2"). Use scraps of many different prints and solids to make the blocks in your quilt sparkle like sunlight through falling leaves.*

 # Autumn

Morning Star

"Fall" into this easy autumn-colored quilt and have some fun!

QUILT SIZE: 78" x 94"

MATERIALS
- Assorted medium and dark print scraps each at least 5 1/2" square and totaling 6 yards
- 3 1/2" yards beige
- 3/4 yard black print for the binding
- 5 1/2" yards backing fabric
- 82" x 98" piece of batting

CUTTING
- Cut 120: 5 1/2" squares, assorted medium and dark prints
- Cut 218: 3 1/2" x 5 1/2" rectangles, assorted medium and dark prints
- Cut 99: 3 1/2" squares, beige
- Cut 792: 2" squares, beige
- Cut 9: 2 1/2" x 44" strips, black print, for the binding

DIRECTIONS
- Draw a diagonal line from corner to corner on the wrong side of each 2" beige square. NOTE: *If you prefer, press the 2" beige squares in half diagonally, wrong side in, instead of marking them.*
- Place a marked square on one corner of a 3 1/2" x 5 1/2" medium or dark print rectangle. Sew on the drawn or pressed line, as shown.

- Press the beige square toward the corner, aligning the edges. Trim the seam allowance to 1/4".

- Repeat for the adjacent corner of the rectangle to make an outer sashing unit, as shown. Make 40. Set them aside.

- In the same manner, sew a marked or pressed 2" beige print square to each corner of a remaining 3 1/2" x 5 1/2" medium or dark print rectangle to make an inner sashing unit, as shown. Make 178.

ASSEMBLY
- Lay out ten 5 1/2" medium and dark print squares alternately with 9 outer sashing units, as shown. Sew them together to make an end row. Make 2.

- Lay out nine 3 1/2" beige squares, 8 inner sashing units and 2 outer sashing units, as shown. Sew them together to make a Row A. Make 11.

Row A

- Lay out ten 5 1/2" medium and dark print squares and 9 inner sashing units, alternating them, as shown. Sew them together to make a Row B. Make 10.

Row B

- Referring to the quilt photo, lay out the A and B rows, alternating them to form rows of stars. Join the rows.
- Sew the end rows to the top and bottom of the quilt, referring to the quilt photo for orientation.
- Finish the quilt as described in the *General Directions*, using the 2 1/2" x 44" black print strips for the binding.

When the first frost crunches underfoot on a crisp fall morning, look to the east to see the "**Morning Star**" (78" x 94"). This scrappy quilt was stitched in autumn colors by Jeanne Poore of Overland Park, Kansas, and machine quilted by Freda Smith. The Morning Star pattern is also known as Vestibule.

Winter
Field of Stars

This simple Four Patch and Star design stitched in Christmas colors says, "Winter."

QUILT SIZE: 74" x 84"
FOUR PATCH BLOCK SIZES:
5" and 3 1/2" square
STAR BLOCK SIZE: 10" square

MATERIALS
- 1/4 yard each of 6 red prints
- 1/4 yard each of 4 gray prints
- 1/4 yard each of 4 green prints
- 1 yard red
- 1 yard light print
- 1 3/4 yards light gray print
- 2 3/4 yards charcoal print
- 2 5/8 yards red plaid
- 6 1/2 yards of backing fabric
- 78" x 88" piece of batting

CUTTING
Cut the lengthwise strips before cutting other pieces from the same yardage.

For the quilt center:
- Cut 1: 3" x 44" strip, from each of 6 red prints
- Cut 17: 5 1/2" squares, charcoal print

For the pieced borders:
- Cut 1: 2 1/4" x 44" strip, from each of 6 red prints
- Cut 3: 4" squares, from each of 4 gray prints
- Cut 6: 6 1/4" squares, assorted gray prints, then cut them in quarters diagonally to yield 24 large triangles
- Cut 3: 4" squares from each of 4 green prints
- Cut 6: 6 1/4" squares, assorted green prints, then cut them in quarters diagonally to yield 24 large triangles
- Cut 12: 6 1/4" squares, light print, then cut them in quarters diagonally to yield 48 large triangles
- Cut 8: 3 3/8" squares, light print, then cut them in half diagonally to yield 16 small triangles

For the Star blocks:
- Cut 4: 5 1/2" squares, red for the centers
- Cut 32: 3" squares, red
- Cut 16: 3" squares, light print
- Cut 16: 3" x 5 1/2" rectangles, light print

Also:
- Cut 2: 5 1/2" x 50" lengthwise strips, red plaid
- Cut 2: 5 1/2" x 60" lengthwise strips, red plaid
- Cut 2: 2" x 50" lengthwise strips, light gray print
- Cut 2: 2" x 60" lengthwise strips, light gray print
- Cut 4: 7" squares, charcoal print
- Cut 2: 8" x 62" lengthwise strips, red plaid
- Cut 2: 8" x 90" lengthwise strips, red plaid
- Cut 8: 2 1/2" x 44" strips, red, for the binding

DIRECTIONS
For the quilt center:
- Stitch two 3" x 44" red print strips, right sides together along their length, to make a pieced panel. Make 3.
- Cut thirty-six 3" slices from the pieced panels, as shown.

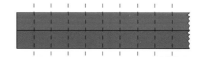

- Stitch 2 slices together to form a large Four Patch block. Make 18.
- Referring to the quilt photo, lay out the 5 1/2" charcoal squares and the large Four Patch blocks in 7 rows of 5.
- Stitch the blocks into rows and join the rows.

For the pieced border:
NOTE: *The quilter color coordinated her pieced borders. Refer to the photo for color placement, or place fabrics randomly for a scrappy look.*
- Lay out 5 green and/or gray large triangles, 4 large light print triangles, and 2 small light print triangles. Stitch the triangles together to make a short inner border. Make 2. Set them aside.

- Lay out 7 large green and/or gray triangles, 6 large light print triangles, and 2 small light print triangles. Stitch the triangles together to make a long inner border. Make 2. Set them aside.
- Stitch two 2 1/4" x 44" red print strips, right sides together along their length, to make a pieced panel. Make 3.
- Cut forty 2 1/4" slices from the panels.
- Stitch 2 slices together to make a small Four Patch block. Make 20.
- Lay out 4 small Four-Patch blocks, five 4" green squares, 5 large green and/or gray triangles, 6 large light print triangles, and 2 small light print triangles.

- Stitch them into diagonal rows and join the rows to make a short outer border. Make 2. Set them aside.
- Lay out 6 small Four Patch blocks, seven 4" green squares, 7 large green and/or gray triangles, 8 large light print triangles, and 2 small light print triangles.

- Stitch them into diagonal rows and join the rows to form a long outer border. Make 2.
- Join a short inner and short outer border to make a short pieced border, as shown. Make 2. Set them aside.

- Join a long inner and an outer border to make a long pieced border. Make 2. Set them aside.

For the Star blocks:
- Draw a diagonal line from corner to corner on the wrong side of each 3" red square.
- Place a marked red square on one end of a 3" x 5 1/2" light print rectangle, right sides together. Sew on the drawn line. Press the red square toward the corner, aligning the edges. Trim the seam allowance to 1/4".
- Place a marked red square on the opposite end of the rectangle. Sew on the drawn line. Press and trim, as before, to make a side unit. Make 16.
- Lay out a 5 1/2" red square, 4 side units, and four 3" light print squares.

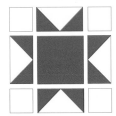

- Stitch them into rows and join the rows to complete a Star block. Make 4. Set them aside.

ASSEMBLY
- Referring to the quilt photo, stitch the short pieced borders to the short sides of the quilt.
- Stitch a long pieced border between 2 Star blocks to make a Star border. Make 2.

*Made in shades of red and green, **"Field of Stars"** (74" x 84") by Linda Taylor of McKinney, Texas, becomes a Christmas-time quilt. It is a perfect pattern for cozy flannels.*

- Stitch the Star borders to the remaining sides of the quilt.
- Stitch a 5 1/2" x 50" red plaid strip to a 2" x 50" light gray print strip, right sides together along their length. Make 2.
- Measure the width of the quilt. Trim the 50" pieced border strips to that measurement. Set them aside.
- Stitch a 5 1/2" x 60" red plaid strip to a 2" x 60" light gray print strip, right sides together along their length. Make 2.
- Measure the length of the quilt. Trim the 60" pieced border strips to that measurement. Sew them to the long sides of the quilt, keeping the red plaid against the quilt.

- Stitch a short pieced border strip between 7" charcoal print squares. Make 2. Stitch them to the remaining sides of the quilt.
- Measure the width of the quilt. Trim the 8" x 62" red plaid strips to that measurement. Stitch them to the short sides of the quilt.
- Measure the length of the quilt, including the borders. Trim the 8" x 90" red plaid strips to that measurement. Stitch them to the remaining sides of the quilt.
- Finish the quilt as described in the *General Directions*, using the 2 1/2" x 44" red strips for the binding.

Winter
The Mitten Tree

Warm your winter by stitching this whimsical quilt.

QUILT SIZE: 51" x 59"
BLOCK SIZE: 4" x 8"

MATERIALS
- Fat quarters (18" x 22") of 15 assorted dark green prints
- 60 assorted bright print scraps, each at least 4" x 7", for the mittens
- Scraps of assorted yellow prints for the star
- 1/4 yard white for the inner border
- 1/2 yard dark green print for the binding
- 3 1/2 yards backing fabric
- 55" x 63" piece of batting

CUTTING
The appliqué pattern is full size and does not include a seam allowance. Make a template for the mitten. Trace around the template on the right side of the fabric and add a 1/8" to 3/16" turn-under allowance when cutting the pieces out. All other dimensions include a 1/4" seam allowance.
- Cut 4: 5" x 9" rectangles from each of 15 assorted dark green prints
- Cut 39: 4 1/2" squares, assorted dark green prints, for the outer border
- Cut 8: 4 1/2" x 5 1/2" rectangles, assorted dark green prints, for the outer border corners
- Cut 4: 1 1/2" squares, assorted dark green prints, for the star block
- Cut 4: 1 7/8" squares, assorted dark green prints, for the star block
- Cut 60: mittens, assorted bright print scraps NOTE: *Reverse the template for half of the mittens.*
- Cut 5: 1 1/2" x 44" strips, white, for the inner border, then cut one of them in half to yield two 1 1/2" x 22" strips
- Cut 8: 1 7/8" squares, assorted yellow prints, for the Star block
- Cut 6: 2 1/2" x 44" strips, dark green

print, for the binding

DIRECTIONS
- Center a bright print mitten on a 5" x 9" dark green print rectangle. Pin it in place. Use the tip of your needle to turn under the allowance as you appliqué the mitten in place to complete a Mitten block.
- Keeping the mitten centered, trim the block to 4 1/2" x 8 1/2". Make 60.
- Referring to the quilt photo for placement ideas, lay out the blocks in 6 rows of 10.
- Stitch the blocks into rows and join the rows.
- Measure the width of the quilt. Trim two 1 1/2" x 44" white strips to that measurement. Sew them to the top and bottom of the quilt.
- Stitch a 1 1/2" x 22" white strip to a 1 1/2" x 44" white strip, end to end, to make a long pieced border. Make 2.
- Measure the length of the quilt. Trim the long pieced borders to that measurement. Stitch them to the sides of the quilt.
- Draw a diagonal line from corner to corner on the wrong side of each of six 1 7/8" assorted yellow print squares. NOTE: *If you prefer, press the 1 7/8" yellow squares in half diagonally, wrong side in, instead of marking them.*
- Lay a marked 1 7/8" yellow print square on a 1 7/8" dark green print square, right sides together. Stitch 1/4" away from the drawn or pressed line on both sides, as shown. Make 4.
- Cut on the marked lines to yield 8 pieced squares. Press the seam allowance toward the dark green print.
- Lay a marked 1 7/8" yellow print square on an unmarked 1 7/8" yellow

print square, right sides together. Stitch 1/4" away from the drawn or pressed line. Make 2. Cut the squares on the marked lines, as before, to yield 4 yellow pieced squares.
- Lay out the pieced squares and four 1 1/2" dark green print squares, as shown. Stitch them into rows and join the rows to complete the Star block.

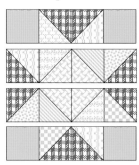

- Referring to the quilt photo, lay out ten 4 1/2" assorted dark green print squares. Stitch them together to make a pieced border. Make 3.
- Stitch a 4 1/2" x 5 1/2" dark green print rectangle to each end of each pieced border. Set one aside.
- Stitch pieced borders to the sides of the quilt.
- Stitch the remaining pieced border to the bottom of the quilt.
- Referring to the quilt photo, lay out the 9 remaining 4 1/2" dark green print squares and the Star block in a row. Stitch them together to make a Star border.
- Stitch a 4 1/2" x 5 1/2" dark green print rectangles to the ends of the Star border, as before.
- Stitch the Star border to the top of the quilt.
- Finish the quilt as described in the *General Directions*, using the 2 1/2" x 44" dark green print strips for the binding.

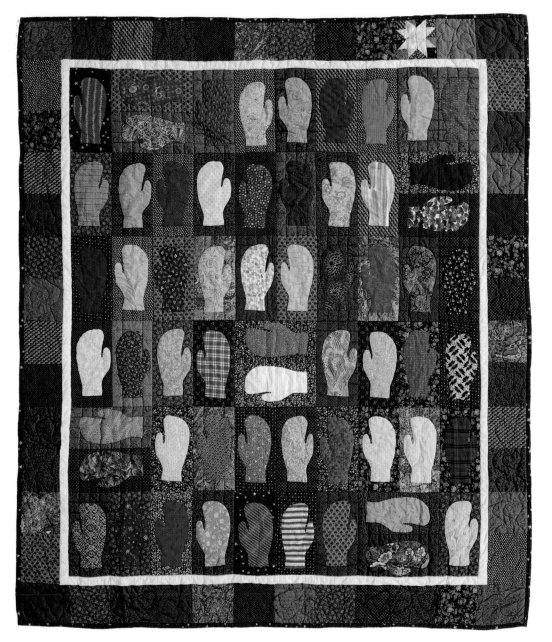

A holiday tradition of decorating Christmas trees with mittens for donations to needy children inspired Virginia Jones of Taunton, Massachusetts, to create **"The Mitten Tree"** *(51" x 59")*. Mittens do not have to come in pairs when you make your version of this delightful wintertime quilt.

Full-size pattern piece for The Mitten Tree.

Winter

Random Stars

*Dark, cold winter nights are perfect for watching—
or sleeping under—constellations of stars.*

QUILT SIZE: 90" x 114"
BLOCK SIZES: 3", 4", 6", 8", 9", and 12"

MATERIALS

• Assorted blue prints totaling 6 1/2 yards
• 6 1/2 yards white
• 3 3/4 yards navy print for the borders and binding
• 8 yards backing fabric
• 94" x 118" piece of batting

CUTTING

Cut the lengthwise navy print strips before cutting other pieces from the same yardage. Group the pieces for each Star block as you cut them.
For each of eleven 12" Star blocks:
• Cut 1: 6 1/2" square, blue print
• Cut 8: 3 1/2" squares, same blue print
For each of three 9" Star blocks:
• Cut 1: 5" square, blue print
• Cut 8: 2 3/4" squares, same blue print
For each of eight 8" Star blocks:
• Cut 1: 4 1/2" square, blue pint
• Cut 8: 2 1/2" squares, same blue print
For each of one hundred eight 6" Star blocks:
• Cut 1: 3 1/2" square, blue print
• Cut 8: 2" squares, same blue print
For each of forty 4" Star blocks:
• Cut 1: 2 1/2" square, blue print
• Cut 8: 1 1/2" squares, same blue print
For each of twenty-one 3" Star blocks:
• Cut 1: 2" square, blue print
• Cut 8: 1 1/4" squares, same blue print
Also:
• Cut 44: 3 1/2" x 6 1/2" rectangles, white, for the 12" blocks

• Cut 44: 3 1/2" squares, white, for the 12" blocks
• Cut 12: 2 3/4" x 5" rectangles, white, for the 9" blocks
• Cut 12: 2 3/4" squares, white, for the 9" blocks
• Cut 32: 2 1/2" x 4 1/2" rectangles, white, for the 8" blocks
• Cut 32: 2 1/2" squares, white, for the 8" blocks
• Cut 432: 2" x 3 1/2" rectangles, white, for the 6" blocks
• Cut 432: 2" squares, white, for the 6" blocks
• Cut 160: 1 1/2" x 2 1/2" rectangles, white, for the 4" blocks
• Cut 160: 1 1/2" squares, white, for the 4" blocks
• Cut 84: 1 1/4" x 2" rectangles, white, for the 3" blocks
• Cut 84: 1 1/4" squares, white, for the 3" blocks
• Cut 2: 3 1/2" x 84 1/2" lengthwise strips, navy print, for the inner border
• Cut 2: 3 1/2" x 66 1/2" lengthwise strips, navy print, for the inner border
• Cut 2: 6" x 105" lengthwise strips, navy print, for the outer border
• Cut 2: 6" x 94" lengthwise strips, navy print, for the outer border
• Cut 11: 2 1/2" x 44" strips, navy print, for the binding

PIECING

For each 12" Star block:
• Working with the pieces cut for one 12" block, draw a diagonal line from corner to corner on the wrong side of each 3 1/2" blue print square. NOTE: *If you prefer, press the 3 1/2" blue print squares in half diagonally, wrong side in,*

instead of marking them.
• Lay a marked square on one end of a 3 1/2" x 6 1/2" white rectangle, right sides together. Sew on the drawn or pressed line. Press the blue print square toward the corner, aligning the edges. Trim the seam allowance to 1/4".
• Lay a marked blue print square on the opposite end of the white rectangle, right sides together. Sew, press and trim as before, to complete a Star point unit. Make 4.
• Lay out the 6 1/2" blue print square, 4 Star point units, and four 3 1/2" white squares. Sew them into rows and join the rows to complete a 12" Star block. Make 11.

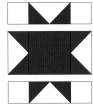

For the 9", 8", 6", 4", and 3" Star blocks:
• Repeat the same procedure using appropriately sized pieces from the cutting list to make three 9" blocks, eight 8" blocks, one hundred eight 6" blocks (52 will be used for the quilt center and 56 for the border), forty 4" blocks, and twenty-one 3" blocks.

ASSEMBLY

• Lay out an 8" block and five 4" blocks. Join them to make a Star unit, as shown. Make 8. Set them aside.

*To express her love of blue, Mary Guggemos of Overland Park, Kansas, stitched "**Random Stars**" (90" x 114") from many different blue fabrics. Six different-sized star blocks are incorporated into this quilt, making it twinkle like stars in a dark winter night sky. Mary drew inspiration for her quilt from an original design by Bea Oglesby, also of Overland Park.*

• Lay out a 9" Star block and seven 3" Star blocks. Join them to make a Star unit, as shown. Make 3. Set them aside.

• Lay out two 6" blocks. Join them to make a double-Star unit, as shown. Make 26. Set 10 aside.

• Lay out 2 double-Star units. Join them to make a Star unit, as shown. Make 8.

• Referring to the Assembly Diagram, lay out the Star units in 7 rows.

• Sew the units into rows and join the rows.

• Sew the 3 1/2" x 84 1/2" navy print strips to the long sides of the quilt.

• Sew the 3 1/2" x 66 1/2" navy print strips to the remaining sides of the quilt.

• Lay out fifteen 6" Star blocks in a row. Sew them together to make a long Star border. Make 2.

• Sew them to the long sides of the quilt.

• Lay out thirteen 6" Star blocks in a row. Sew them together to make a short Star border. Make 2.

• Sew them to the short sides of the quilt.

• Measure the length of the quilt. Trim the 6" x 105" navy print strips to that measurement. Sew them to the long sides of the quilt.

• Measure the width of the quilt, including the borders. Trim the 6" x 94" navy print strips to that measurement. Sew them to the short sides of the quilt.

• Finish the quilt as described in the *General Directions*, using the 2 1/2" x 44" navy print strips for the binding.

Assembly Diagram

Maple Leaf

(continued from page 18)

ASSEMBLY

• Stitch a 2 1/2" x 12 1/2" brown sashing strip to the left side of each Maple Leaf block, as shown.

• Referring to the Assembly Diagram, lay out the Maple Leaf blocks on point, the remaining 2 1/2" x 12 1/2" brown sashing strips, the long 2 1/2" brown sashing strips, off-white setting triangles, and off-white corner triangles.

• Beginning at the upper left hand corner, stitch a 2 1/2" x 12 1/2" brown sashing strip to the upper right side of the Maple Leaf block. Center and stitch a 2 1/2" x 20" brown sashing strip to the upper left side of the block. Trim the ends even with the sides of the block, as shown.

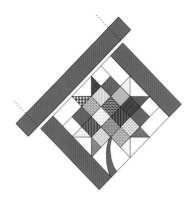

• Stitch 2 off-white setting triangles and an off-white corner triangle to the sides and top of the block, as shown. Repeat the process using the lower right block in the layout. Return the pieced units to opposite corners of the layout.

• Stitch the next row, joining 3 Maple Leaf blocks. Stitch a 2 1/2" x 12 1/2" brown sashing strip to the right end of the row. Center and stitch a 2 1/2" x 48" brown sashing strip to the top of the row. Trim the ends even with the blocks. Sew an off-white setting triangle to each end to make a pieced section. Return the section to the layout.

• Referring to the Assembly Diagram, stitch the remaining blocks, sashing strips, and setting triangles into sections.

• Join the sections. Stitch the remaining off-white corner triangles to the remaining corners of the quilt.

• Finish the quilt as described in the *General Directions,* using the 2 1/2" x 44" off-white strips for the binding.

Assembly Diagram

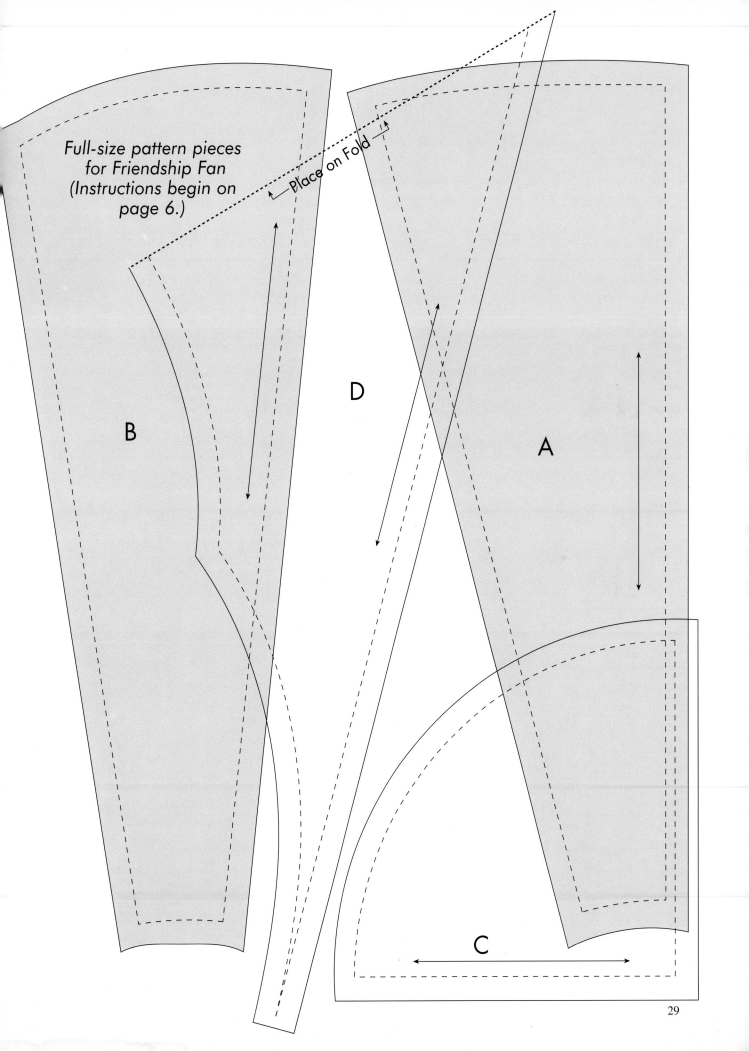

Full-size pattern pieces for Friendship Fan (Instructions begin on page 6.)

Place on Fold

B

D

A

C

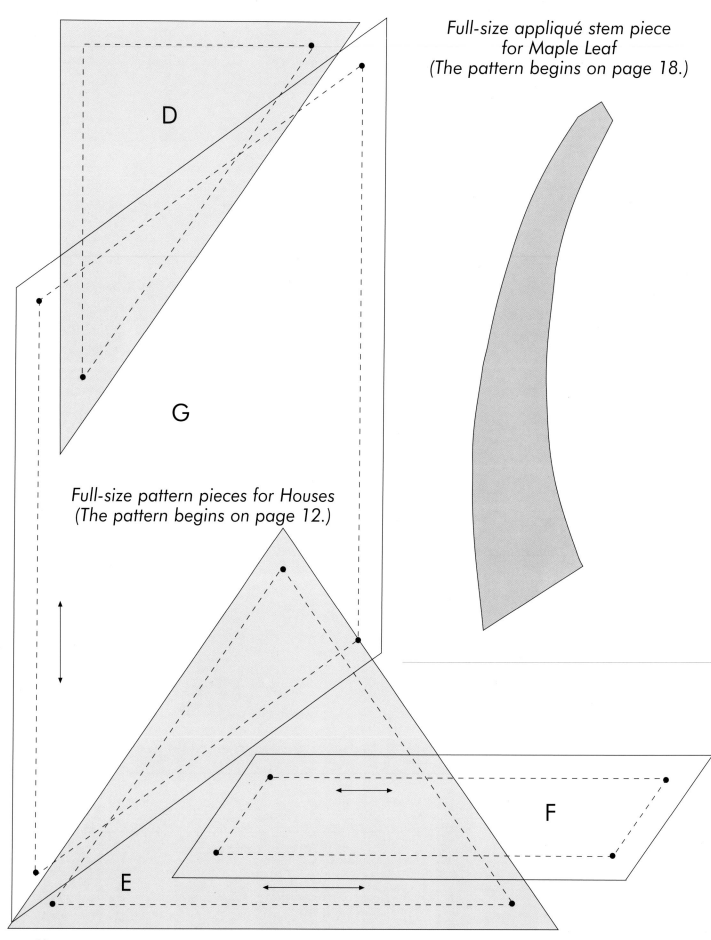

*Full-size appliqué stem piece
for Maple Leaf
(The pattern begins on page 18.)*

D

G

*Full-size pattern pieces for Houses
(The pattern begins on page 12.)*

E

F

General Directions

ABOUT THE PATTERNS

Read through the pattern directions before cutting fabric for your quilt. Yardage requirements are based on 44" fabric with a useable width of 42". Pattern directions are given in step-by-step order.

FABRICS

We suggest using 100% cotton. Wash fabrics in warm water with mild detergent and no fabric softener. Wash darks separately and check for bleeding during the rinse cycle. Dry fabric on a warm-to-hot setting to shrink it. Press with hot dry iron to remove any wrinkles.

ROTARY CUTTING

Begin by folding the fabric in half, selvage to selvage. Make sure the selvages are even and the folded edge is smooth. Fold the fabric in half again, bringing the fold and the selvages together, again making sure everything is smooth and flat.

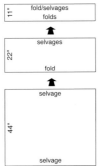

Position the folded fabric on a cutting mat so that the fabric extends to the right for right-handed people, or to the left for left-handed people. (Mats with grid lines are recommended because the lines serve as guides to help ensure the cut strips will be straight.)

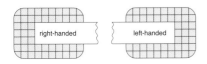

Lay the fabric so that the folded edge is along one of the horizontal lines on the mat. Place the ruler on one of the vertical lines, just over the uneven edges of the fabric. The ruler must be absolutely perpendicular to the folded edge. Trim the uneven edges with a rotary cutter. Make a clean cut through the fabric, beginning in front of the folds and cutting through to the opposite edge with one clean (not short and choppy) stroke. Always cut away from yourself—never

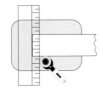

toward yourself!

Move the ruler to the proper width for cutting the first strip, and continue cutting until you have the required number of strips. To keep the cut edges even, always move the ruler, not the fabric. Open up one fabric strip and check the spots where there were folds. If the fabric was not evenly lined up or the ruler was incorrectly positioned, there will be a bend at each of the folds in the fabric.

When cutting many strips, check after every four or five strips to make sure the strips are straight. Leave the other strips folded in fourths until you are ready to use them.

TEMPLATES

Template patterns are full size and, unless otherwise noted, include a 1/4" seam allowance as do all dimensions given. The solid line is the cutting line; the dashed line is the stitching line. An "R" following the letter means the piece must be reversed. Place a sheet of firm, clear plastic over the patterns and trace the cutting line and/or stitching line for each one. Templates for machine piecing include seam allowances, templates for hand piecing generally do not. Templates for appliqué never include seam allowances. Use a permanent marker to record the name and size of block, the grainline, and number of pieces needed for one block on every template.

MARKING FABRIC

Test marking tools for removability before using them. Sharpen pencils often. Align the grainline on the template with the grainline of the fabric. Place a piece of fine sandpaper beneath the fabric to prevent slipping, if desired. For machine piecing, mark the right side of the fabric. Unless otherwise noted, for hand piecing mark the wrong side and flip all directional (asymmetrical) templates before tracing them. Mark and cut just enough pieces to make a sample block. Piece the block to be sure the templates are accurate. Handle bias edges carefully to avoid stretching them.

When marking for appliqué, trace the templates on the right side of the fabric. Leave at least a 3/8" space between hand appliqué templates to allow for a 1/8" to 3/16" turn-under allowance. Cut

directly on the traced line for machine appliqué.

PIECING

For machine piecing, sew 12 stitches per inch, exactly 1/4" from the edge of the fabric. If desired, mark the throat plate with a piece of masking tape 1/4" away from the point where the needle pierces the fabric. Start and stop stitching at the cut edges unless otherwise noted. Backstitching is not necessary unless specified in the pattern.

For hand piecing, begin with a small backstitch. Continue with a small running stitch, backstitching every 3-4 stitches. Stitch directly on the marked line from point to point, not edge to edge.

APPLIQUÉ

Mark the position of the pieces on the background. If the fabric is light, lay it over the pattern, matching centers and other indicators. Trace these marks lightly. If the fabric is dark, use a light box or other light source to make tracing easier. To hand appliqué, baste or pin appliqué pieces to the background block in stitching order. Use a blindstitch or buttonhole stitch to appliqué the pieces. Do not turn under or stitch any edges that will lie under other pieces.

To machine appliqué, baste pieces in place with a long machine basting stitch or a narrow, open zigzag stitch. Then stitch over the basting with a short, wide satin stitch. Placing a piece of paper between the wrong side of the fabric and the feed dogs of the sewing machine will help stabilize the fabric. Carefully remove excess paper when stitching is complete.

PRESSING

Press with a dry iron. Press seam allowances toward the darker of the two pieces whenever possible. Otherwise, trim away 1/16" from the darker seam allowance to prevent it from showing through. Press all blocks, sashings, and borders before assembling the quilt top. Press appliqué blocks from the wrong side, on a towel, to prevent a flat, shiny look.

MITERED BORDERS

Cut border strips the length specified in the pattern. Match the center of the quilt top with the center of the border strip and pin to the corners. Stitch, beginning, ending, and backstitching each seamline 1/4" from the edge of the quilt top. After all borders have been attached, miter one corner at a time. With the quilt top right side down, lay one border over the other. Draw a straight line at a 45° angle from the inner to the outer corner.

Reverse the positions of the borders and mark another corner-to-corner line. With the borders right sides together and the marked seamlines carefully matched, stitch from the inner to the outer corner. Open the mitered seam to make sure it lies flat, then trim the excess fabric and press the seam open.

FINISHING YOUR QUILT: MARKING QUILTING LINES

Mark the quilt top before basting it together with the batting and backing. Chalk pencils show well on dark fabrics; otherwise use a very hard (#3 or #4) pencil or other marker for this purpose. Test your marker for removability first. Transfer paper designs by placing fabric over the design and tracing. A light box may be necessary for darker fabrics. Precut plastic stencils that fit the area you wish to quilt may be placed on top of the quilt and traced. Use a ruler to mark straight, even grids.

Outline quilting does not require marking. Simply eyeball 1/4" from the seam or stitch "in the ditch" next to the seam or the neighboring patch. To prevent uneven stitching, try to avoid quilting through seam allowances wherever possible.

Masking tape can also be used to mark straight lines. Temporary quilting stencils can be made from clear adhesive-backed paper or freezer paper and reused many times. To avoid residue, do not leave tape or adhesive-backed paper on the quilt overnight.

BASTING

Cut the batting and backing at least 2" larger than the quilt top on all sides. Tape the backing, wrong side up, on a flat surface to anchor it. Smooth the batting on top, followed by the quilt top, right side up. Baste the three layers together to form a quilt sandwich. Begin at the center and baste horizontally,

then vertically. Add more lines of basting approximately every 6" until the entire top is secured.

QUILTING

Quilting is done with a short, strong needle called a "between." The lower the number (size) of the needle, the larger it is. Begin with an 8 or 9 and progress to a size 10 or 12. Use a thimble on the middle finger of the hand that pushes the needle. Begin quilting at the center of the quilt and work outward to keep the tension even and quilting smooth.

Using an 18" length of quilting thread knotted at one end, insert the needle through the quilt top only and bring it up exactly where you will begin. Pop the knot through the fabric to bury it in the batting. Push the needle with the thimbled finger of the upper hand and slightly depress the fabric in front of the needle with the thumb. Redirect the needle back to the top of the quilt using the middle or index finger of the lower hand.

Repeat with each stitch, using a rocking motion. Finish by knotting the thread close to the surface and popping the knot through the fabric to bury it in the batting layer. Remove basting when all the quilting is done.

If you wish to machine quilt, we recommend consulting one of the many excellent books available on that subject.

BINDING

Trim the excess batting and backing even to within 1/4" of the raw edge of the quilt top. Cut binding strips with the grain for straight-edge quilts. To make 1/2" finished binding, cut 2 1/2"-wide strips. Sew strips together with diagonal seams; trim and press the seams open.

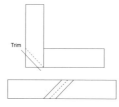

Fold the strip in half lengthwise, wrong side in, and press. Position the strip on the right side of the quilt top, aligning the raw edges of the binding with the edge of the quilt top, (not so

that all raw edges are even). Leaving 6" free and beginning at least 8" from one corner, stitch the binding to the quilt with a 1/2" seam allowance measuring from the raw edge of the backing. When you reach a corner, stop stitching 1/2" from the edge and backstitch. Clip thread and remove the quilt from the machine. Fold the binding up and away from the quilt, forming a 45° angle as shown.

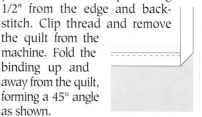

Keeping the angled folds secure, fold the binding back down. This fold should be even with the edge of the quilt top. Begin stitching at the fold.

Continue stitching around the quilt in this manner to within 6" of the starting point. To finish, fold both strips back along the edge of the quilt so that the folded edges meet about 3" from both lines of stitching and the binding lies flat on the quilt. Finger press to crease the folds. Cut both strips 1 1/4" from the folds.

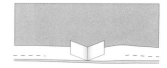

Open both strips and place the ends at right angles to each other, right sides together. Fold the bulk of the quilt out of your way. Join the strips with a diagonal seam, as shown.

Trim the seam allowance to 1/4" and press it open. Refold the joined strip wrong side in. Place the binding flat against the quilt and finish stitching it to the quilt. Trim the layers as needed so that the binding edge will be filled with batting when you fold the binding to the back of the quilt. Blindstitch the binding to the back, covering the seamline. Make a label containing pertinent information and attach it to the back of your quilt.